Original title:
Laughing Under Larch Limbs

Copyright © 2025 Creative Arts Management OÜ
All rights reserved.

Author: Colin Harrington
ISBN HARDBACK: 978-1-80567-379-8
ISBN PAPERBACK: 978-1-80567-678-2

Serenity Amidst the Swaying Pines

Beneath the swaying branches high,
The whispers of the wind pass by.
A squirrel dances, oh so spry,
While humor flits like clouds in the sky.

Shadows play on the forest floor,
As laughter echoes, hearts explore.
Each crack and creak brings smiles galore,
In this tranquil hideaway, we adore.

Merriment in the Forest's Heart

In the heart where the wild things roam,
A jester leaps, feels right at home.
With a grin wide as the river's foam,
The trees join in, a leafy poem.

Bouncing beasts, in playful chase,
Each twist and turn, a merry race.
In every nook, a happy face,
Nature's stage, a charming place.

Jests Beneath the Boughs

Between the roots where tall grass sways,
The crickets chirp their comical plays.
Giggling leaves in a sunlit blaze,
Turn simple moments into festive days.

A raccoon peeks with a wink so sly,
As playful breezes flutter by.
Life's little jokes, oh my, oh my,
Beneath the boughs, spirits fly.

Nature's Giggle in the Glade

In the glade where sunlight twirls,
The day unfolds as laughter swirls.
With every bounce, a joy unfurls,
In nature's charm, the world whirls.

Mirthful whispers of branches sway,
As shadows gather to join the play.
Each moment brightens, come what may,
Nature's giggle lights the way.

Laughter Like a Soft Breeze

A giggle floats on gentle air,
As leaves rustle without a care.
Squirrels prance and chase their tails,
While sunlight weaves through leafy trails.

Chirping birds join in the cheer,
Their songs spread joy that we can hear.
The world is bright, with smiles all round,
In nature's hug, our hearts are found.

Tickled by the Sunbeams

Sunbeams dance on berry patches,
Tickles from the sunlight catches.
Children giggle 'neath the sky,
Chasing butterflies that flutter by.

A jester squirrel dons a cap,
While seeking acorns for a nap.
With every bounce and playful leap,
The forest laughs, no time for sleep.

Dancing in the Dappled Light

Twinkling spots of light do swirl,
As creatures play, their tails unfurl.
A rabbit hops with nimble grace,
In this vibrant, joyous place.

The shadows play hide and seek,
With every laugh, we softly peek.
In this moment, time stands still,
With every giggle, hearts are filled.

Whimsy in the Wilderness

In forests where the wild things play,
Whimsy rules both night and day.
A fox in stripes, a hare in shoes,
Every step a funny muse.

Tall oaks sway, whispering jokes,
Unraveling laughter among the folks.
With every twist in nature's page,
We find joy that warms our age.

The Sound of Smiles in Nature's Loung

In the shade where giggles bloom,
Whispers dance, dispelling gloom.
Squirrels chatter in playful jest,
As sunshine warms the forest's chest.

Breezes tickle the branches high,
While clouds float lazily by.
Nature hums a merry tune,
Beneath the friendly, watchful moon.

Playful Spirits Amidst the Sturdy

Beneath the giants, laughter weaves,
As every twig and leaf believes.
Tiny feet scamper with delight,
Creating joy that feels just right.

Echoes of joy fill the air,
Bouncing high without a care.
Frogs perform their silly show,
Jumping high amid the flow.

Cheerful Revelations in the Leafy Veil

Sunbeams peek through emerald screens,
Casting shadows of playful scenes.
Each twist of branch brings laughter's call,
As critters play and never fall.

Jokes exchanged by feathered friends,
A chorus of chuckles that never ends.
With every rustle, spirits rise,
In nature's laughter, joy lies.

Glee Cascades from Branch to Ground

Ripples of joy flow down the bark,
Where playful winks light up the dark.
Animals gather, ears all perked,
In this sanctuary where giggles lurked.

Along the path, footsteps dance,
In whimsical rhythms, hearts enhance.
The world spins with a chuckling breeze,
As happiness flutters through the trees.

Frolics in the Leafy Abode

In a grove where shadows play,
Joyful voices fill the day,
Squirrels dance, a jolly sight,
Chasing tails in pure delight.

With every twist and silly cheer,
Happiness is drawn quite near,
A picnic spread with treats galore,
Laughter spills from every pore.

Tickling leaves that gently sway,
Echoes of mirth lead the way,
Beneath the branches, friends unite,
In this realm of pure delight.

As the day drifts into dusk,
With silly games and playful husk,
The moonlight joins the merry scene,
Crafting smiles from what has been.

Dappled Sunlight and Spontaneous Smiles

Bright beams dance on the forest floor,
A greet of sunshine, who could ask for more?
Birds above sing silly tunes,
As shadows weave like playful goons.

Children's laughter fills the air,
With giggles tossed upon the dare,
A broomstick horse gallops by,
Chasing dreams with giddy sighs.

Breezes whisper playful pranks,
As butterflies join in the ranks,
They flutter by with grace and flair,
As if to tease the world's cold stare.

Grins get wider; joy extends,
In this place where laughter bends,
Every moment a treasure's find,
Where silliness is simply kind.

Laughter's Echo in the Woodland

Footsteps crunch through crisp, dry leaves,
As giggles float among the eaves,
A fox peeks out, a curious friend,
Sharing chuckles 'round the bend.

Under boughs, the shadows tease,
Adventures wait with playful breeze,
Jumping over roots and stones,
Echoes carry happy tones.

Silly hats and flower crowns,
Swaying merrily like silly clowns,
With every leap and friendly call,
Nature beckons, come one, come all!

As daylight fades and stars ignite,
We share our tales in joyful night,
With twinkling eyes, we gladly share,
A tapestry of love and care.

Nature's Carnival Under the Trees

A circus blooms beneath the sky,
With vibrant laughter floating high,
Acrobatic squirrels in a whirl,
Juggling acorns, watch them twirl!

The sunbeams twinkle, spirits rise,
Revelers dance, the world their prize,
Every giggle a melody sweet,
A woodland fair where hearts can meet.

Shapes and shadows, brightly cast,
As silly masks float flying fast,
The trees alight with glimmering cheer,
Encircling joy that draws us near.

With every twinkle of the night,
We share our dreams, our hearts take flight,
And in this realm, so wild and free,
Mirth and magic weave a spree.

Banter Beneath the Swirling Green

In shadows where the breezes play,
Squirrels chatter, stealing the day.
With acorns tossed like silly dreams,
A playful jest in nature beams.

Twisting trunks with faces wide,
A chorus sings of woodland pride.
Mischief dances on leaves afloat,
As giggles spring from a feathered throat.

Footfalls echo, laughter trails,
A jester's song fills leafy veils.
Whimsical sights blossom in glee,
The forest holds its jubilee.

In every nook, a joke awaits,
As nature spins her charming fates.
Beneath the green, we play our part,
With wit that tickles the wild heart.

The Forest's Hidden Laughter

Amidst the trees where shadows peek,
The woodland whispers secrets cheek.
  Twisted roots and branches sway,
  They weave a tale of bright array.

From dappled leaves, a giggle leaps,
As woodland creatures play for keeps.
  Frogs croak tales of fishy fun,
  While rabbits race; the day's a run.

  Clouds above like cotton feet,
  Dance with joy, a rhythmic beat.
Each breeze carries chuckles low,
  A serenade from friend to foe.

Secrets shared in rustling sighs,
As trees exchange their joyful cries.
  In fairy glades where spirits play,
The heart finds warmth on this fine day.

Tranquil Chuckles Beneath the Sky

Beneath the vast and cotton sky,
A symphony of whimsy flies.
Gentle breezes stir the ground,
In this haven, joy abounds.

Giggling flowers in sun's embrace,
Swirling petals, a bright chase.
Butterflies in dizzy twirls,
Join in laughter, dances whirl.

Crisp green blades beneath our toes,
Nature's comedy always shows.
Whether prancing or in stoops,
Every moment prompts our whoops.

As twilight glimmers, shadows play,
The stars ignite in bright array.
Here in this shock of wonder,
We find the light, sweet jokes to ponder.

Joyful Whispers Through the Bark

Amidst the trunks, where hush resides,
A sprinkle of charm in each stride.
Sapling secrets softly spill,
With chuckles bubbling, hearts they fill.

Curled roots with stories tightly bound,
Echoing laughter in the ground.
Mirthful breezes twist and shout,
As nature's jokes weave in and out.

Above, the canopies engage,
In playful sparring, wisdom sage.
Leaves rustle with a choir's cheer,
Inviting all to linger near.

In this embrace, the world feels right,
With laughter chasing off the night.
In every whisper, joy we find,
A shared smirk in the forest kind.

The Laughter of Leaves

Green hats dance in the breeze,
Branches sway with such ease.
Squirrels chatter in delight,
While shadows play hide and seek at night.

Breezes tickle the blades of grass,
As funny faces in the glass.
Nature chuckles, birds a-whirl,
In this whimsical, playful swirl.

Each rustle tells a joke anew,
With blossoms nodding, as if they knew.
Sunbeams join the merry jest,
In this green grove, we feel our best.

Giggling petals drop like rain,
While laughter echoes, soft and plain.
The forest hums a silly song,
Inviting us to sing along.

Joyful Gathering in the Glade

Bright clouds float on a sunny day,
Flowers laugh in their own way.
Bumblebees buzz with a grin,
Spreading joy from within.

Mushrooms share their cheeky tales,
While the wind carries silly gales.
Dancing shadows leap and twirl,
As nature's laughter starts to unfurl.

Rustling leaves play tag in flight,
Breezes whisper secrets, light.
Children's giggles rise like steam,
In this friendly, sunlit dream.

Every step brings blissful sound,
In this gathering, joy is found.
Together we partake in glee,
In the glade where all are free.

Echoing Chuckles in the Thicket

Jokes abound in the underbrush,
Where shadows play and colors rush.
A fox grins with a sly intent,
As curtains of leaves slowly bend.

Squirrels race on a playful spree,
Chasing each other, wild and free.
Echoes bounce from tree to tree,
In this lively spree of jubilee.

Crickets join the merry band,
With chirps that tickle, soft and grand.
Thickets hide the merriest of sights,
Where laughter lives on starry nights.

The laughter swells, a joyful tide,
With nature as our laughing guide.
We dance in shadows, twirl with cheer,
In this thicket, we lose all fear.

Whispers of Happiness in the Woods

Whispers of joy flutter through trees,
Carried softly on the breeze.
Tiny critters hold a feast,
Sharing giggles, never ceased.

Swaying grasses nod in cheer,
As playful spirits gather near.
The sun peeks through like a prankster,
Making shadows twist and linger.

Delightful sounds fill the air,
While dancing leaves sway without care.
Branches tickle, roots embrace,
In the woods, we find our place.

Joyful whispers quilt the night,
As fireflies twinkle, oh so bright.
Nature's laughter, winks and bliss,
In this world, we find our kiss.

Delightful Whispers in the Understory

Beneath the branches, giggles flow,
Where shadows dance and breezes blow.
A squirrel twirls, a playful sight,
While mushrooms laugh in morning light.

The ferns do sway, a gentle tease,
As sunlight plays among the trees.
A curious owl, with knowing eyes,
Joins in the fun, no need for lies.

As butterflies flit, their colors bright,
They tease the bees, in sheer delight.
Nature's choir sings out in glee,
Whispering secrets, wild and free.

Joyful Raindrops on the Canopy

Pitter-patter on leafy crowns,
Nature giggles, wide grins abound.
Each drop a joke that falls from height,
Creating laughter, pure and bright.

The worms rejoice in muddy pools,
While frogs play leap, breaking the rules.
With every splash, a jest is made,
In vibrant hues, the forest played.

Raindrops race down tree's tall frame,
A playful chase, a joyful game.
Under the boughs, wild chuckles rise,
As nature winks with twinkling eyes.

Lighthearted Moments in the Sylvan Realm

In the glen where shadows dance,
Mischief hide and laughter prance.
A rabbit hops, with ears so grand,
While tree trunks twist, as if they planned.

With whispers soft and tickled leaves,
The woodland joins in hearty heaves.
As squirrels chatter, making noise,
Their antics spark such childish joys.

The sun peeks through, a bright surprise,
Making sparkles through the skies.
All around, the mirth does bloom,
Filling the air with light and room.

Swaying Together in Nature's Embrace

Amidst tall trees where laughter stirs,
The gentle breeze, it softly purrs.
A dance of shadows, a giggling spree,
As nature twirls, wild and free.

The brook joins in with splashes bright,
While critters scamper, hearts alight.
In secret nooks, the whispers play,
Creating mischief in their own way.

With every sway and every sound,
Joy intertwines, so richly bound.
Together here, where cheer is found,
In nature's arms, we spin around.

Blissful Moments Amidst the Foliage

In the shade of the large green tree,
Children giggle, wild and free.
They chase the shadows, swift and bright,
As leaves dance down in playful light.

A jester's hat upon a head,
With silly pranks that laughter spread.
The branches sway, a gentle sway,
As nature plays its grand ballet.

Sweet cookies shared and tales exchanged,
With every joke, the mood is changed.
This blissful space, a cheerful nest,
In nature's arms, we feel the best.

Sunbeams filter through the green,
Creating scenes that feel serene.
For in this place, we find our song,
Where all our hearts and laughs belong.

Contentment in Nature's Embrace

The sun peeks through with a wink so sly,
While ants march by, as if to fly.
A picnic spread, a feast for all,
And nearby, a squirrel does a high-stakes crawl.

With every bite, a chuckle bursts,
At strange bird calls and the pines' soft thirsts.
Nature's humor, a comic play,
As clouds form shapes that drift away.

Daisies twirl in the gentle breeze,
Tickling toes with utmost ease.
We cherish this sweet, vivid scene,
In moments where we're truly keen.

The path ahead is overgrown,
Yet laughter echoes, never alone.
With friends to share each silly jest,
In nature's arms, we feel the best.

Smiles Beneath the Boughs

Beneath the branches, shadows play,
With giggles echoing all the way.
A game of tag with friends so dear,
Each bounce and stumble brings a cheer.

A butterfly flits, as if to tease,
While we fall down, craft stories with ease.
In tangled roots we find our fun,
As knots of laughter come undone.

With pie on faces and hay in hair,
The joy we share fills all the air.
A symphony of chuckles rings,
As happy hearts take to the swings.

The sun dips low, our time draws tight,
But here we bask in this delight.
For under these boughs, we feel alive,
A place where purest giggles thrive.

Memories Made in the Meadow

In the meadow where daisies sway,
We weave our stories, come what may.
With laughter intertwined in every thread,
Each spoken jest a joy to spread.

A kite takes flight, a colorful sight,
While clouds compete in their fluffy flight.
We chase our dreams with every yell,
In this bright space where spirits swell.

With pets around, noses twitch and play,
Their antics spice up the sunny day.
Friendships blossom like flowers in bloom,
Creating joy that fills the room.

As twilight whispers the day goodbye,
We carry smiles beneath the sky.
In this meadow, memories are born,
With warmth of laughter forever worn.

Frolic in the Forest Fires

Tiny feet dazzle on the ground,
Whispers of laughter, a playful sound.
Squirrels dance, their tails a blur,
A frolicsome chase, oh what a stir!

Beneath the boughs, a game of hide,
Giggles spill forth, they can't abide.
Jumping through shadows, quick as can be,
Nature's jesters, wild and free.

Branches sway with a rhythmic glee,
Together they prance, just you and me.
An impish breeze tugs at our clothes,
We tumble and roll, where mischief flows.

Candles of sunlight, all aglow,
Chasing the sunbeams, to and fro.
With nature's charm, our spirits soar,
In the heart of the forest, we laugh some more.

Joyful Bonds Amidst the Bark

Whispers of joy echo between,
Friends entwined, a festive scene.
Laughter spills from each gnarled tree,
In every nook, pure jubilee.

With silly hats made of leaves and twine,
They prance about, feeling divine.
As shadows dance in playful sway,
We toast to the quirks of this fine day.

Frogs croak songs, a quirky tune,
Raccoons join in, beneath the moon.
Giggles burst like bubbles in air,
Moments cherished, free from care.

Amidst the bark, we find our way,
Creating memories, bright as day.
With every laugh, the bonds grow tight,
Joyful hearts in the soft twilight.

Whimsy and Wonder in the Wilderness

In the wildwood where the whimsy glows,
Every creature puts on a show.
A deer trips over a gnarled root,
The forest rings with merry hoot!

Bushy tails and twinkling eyes,
Painted skies in a dainty guise.
With each rustle, a surprise awaits,
In this realm of magical fates.

Dancing fireflies with lights so bright,
Draw the stars down, a sparkling night.
Raccoons giggle, than share a snack,
In the heart of strange, they've got no lack.

Through ferny paths, we weave and glide,
Chasing joy on this whimsical ride.
With wonder wrapped in every beam,
Life's a jest, a delightful dream.

Sun Sosaties in the Twisting Limbs

Twisted branches reach and play,
With shadows on this brightening day.
We skewer thoughts like sunny treats,
Dancing in rhythm, our laughter beats.

Sun sosaties on the grill,
Mirthful chats give the heart a thrill.
As smoke curls up in the golden light,
Stories twine till it's day from night.

Each morsel grilled with joy so sweet,
A feast of laughter, a friend's heartbeat.
Nature serves up funny delights,
In twisting limbs, joy ignites.

Through the rustling leaves, a giggle flows,
As friends abound wherever one goes.
With sun-kissed laughter and heart so bold,
Life's grilling flavors never grow cold.

Uproarious Echoes in the Timberland

In the shade where shadows dance,
A squirrel steals a fleeting glance.
He's tripped upon a twiggy mess,
With acorns rolling, what a dress!

Birds chirp witty jokes so bright,
As deer prance in a comical flight.
A raccoon winks with cheeky flair,
To tickle the lively woodland air.

Mushrooms giggle in close-knit rings,
While frogs croak out the best of flings.
The breeze carries a playful tune,
As laughter echoes 'neath the moon.

So gather round, let silliness grow,
In leafy realms where whimsies flow.
Each tree holds tales of joy and cheer,
In this fun-filled forest we revere.

Delightful Murmurs of the Forest Floor

Upon the ground, the creatures greet,
With tiny paws in rhythmic beat.
A chipmunk rolls, his cheeks so wide,
Nature's jesters, oh, what a ride!

Leaves rustle with cheeky delight,
As rabbits hop into the light.
A stoic owl shakes off the gloom,
In playful antics, he finds his room.

The brook bubbles with secrets untold,
While dragonflies dance, bright and bold.
In every corner, joy takes its place,
With smiles that light up every space.

So let the giggles bounce and soar,
In the heart of the woods where spirits explore.
A symphony of fun in the sunbeam glow,
Where every nook sets laughter aglow.

Skits and Smiles in Nature's Arena

Beneath the arch of branches high,
The rabbits trade jokes 'til they cry.
A playful wind sets hats askew,
As nature's jesters take their cue.

A hedgehog twirls with quite a flair,
While foxes lounge without a care.
The pinecones giggle as they drop,
In this arena, no one can stop!

Owls pull faces, wise yet silly,
While shadowy figures make us willy-nilly.
With every rustle, the forest grins,
As mischief fills the air like spins.

Let's dance upon this earthy stage,
Engage in fun, forget the age.
For here, in nature's vibrant spread,
Laughter blooms where all fears tread.

Euphoria Among the Ancient Trees

In the embrace of branches old,
Where secrets of the forest are told.
A bear does a jig, what a sight!
Joy spills forth, sprinkled with light.

The sunbeams play games of hide and seek,
While elves peek out, a bit of a tweak.
A bobcat sneezes, it's quite the surprise,
And everyone erupts in merriment skies.

Under the canopy, stories collide,
With crunching leaves like laughter's tide.
Each moment bursts like bubbles of cheer,
In this glacier of joy, we hold dear.

So let's toast to trees and laughter grand,
In this realm where smiles are unplanned.
With every rustle and playful tease,
Euphoria reigns among ancient trees.

Children of the Earth at Play

In fields where daisies twirl and sway,
Kids dance with shadows, bright and gay.
They chase the breeze with eager feet,
Giggles erupt where the sunbeams meet.

With sticks as swords and hats of leaves,
They conquer kingdoms, kings, and thieves.
A game of tag at nature's door,
Each laugh a promise, a vibrant score.

Morning dew joins the lively sound,
While ants march by, all homeward bound.
A puddle splash becomes a cheer,
Nature's playground, forever near.

In corners green, the merriment flows,
Joy spills over, as friendship grows.
With every leap, a tale is spun,
In earth's embrace, they bask in fun.

Joyous Encounters in Nature's Studio

Amidst the pines, a canvas wide,
Children paint with laughter, side by side.
Squirrels scamper, what a sight,
Sharing secrets in morning light.

With each bright flower, they weave a tale,
Of wiggly worms on a climbing trail.
The sun tosses gold on their merry play,
Chasing clouds that drift away.

A curious rabbit hops with glee,
Joining the fun as wild as can be.
They mimic the wind, swaying like trees,
Creating joy with the buzzing bees.

And as day fades to twilight's embrace,
They gather joy in this sacred space.
In nature's heart, laughter rings clear,
An eternal dance that draws them near.

The Art of Happiness Beneath the Canopy

Beneath the arch of leaves so bright,
Children craft their world of light.
With painted rocks and sticks for cheer,
Their canvas stretches far and near.

Whimsical creatures join their game,
Each sound a call, each laugh a flame.
They race the breeze, hearts full of fun,
Underneath the laughing sun.

Rustling whispers in the trees,
The wind adds notes to their melodies.
Even the clouds seem to sway,
Dancing along in their quirky play.

As twilight paints the sky with hues,
They gather memories, like morning dew.
In the woodland's arms, joy takes flight,
A masterpiece that dazzles the night.

Woodland Whimsies and Whispers

In a glen where shadows leap and glide,
Children's laughter is a joyful tide.
They chase the sunbeams, quick and spry,
While butterflies flutter and jellybeans fly.

With pinecone hats and grass-stippled shoes,
Adventures unfold in the colorful hues.
They stumble on roots, then giggle aloud,
Nature applauding, a whimsical crowd.

A mischievous fox plays hide and seek,
While team of frogs croak a tune, unique.
These woodland chums share secrets untold,
In a world of wonder, bright and bold.

As stars awaken, the fireflies glow,
Crafting a wonderland, a radiant show.
Here, beneath boughs, smiles brightly play,
In the magic of night, they dream away.

Amusement Among the Needle-clad Arms

In the shade where shadows play,
Bright-eyed critters dance away.
Branches sway with a giggle and spin,
Nature's jesters, a merry din.

Acorns fall with a playful thud,
As squirrels chase with a carefree bud.
Frogs croak a tune in crooked glee,
While birds exchange their jests for free.

Laughter echoes, a swirling breeze,
With whispers between the swaying trees.
Joy unravels in the dappled light,
As woodland spirits take their flight.

The Whimsy of the Woodland Realm

In the glade where the whimsy grows,
Frolicking fawns strike a pose.
With twirls and leaps, they tease the air,
While shadows play in a world so rare.

Dappling sunbeams, they wink and cheer,
As a playful wind draws laughter near.
Flowers nod with a silly wink,
As butterflies swirl, they frolic and blink.

A hare hops by with a wink and a grin,
Chasing its tail with a cheeky spin.
Each rustle and cackle, a joke well told,
In this wondrous realm, forever bold.

A Symphony of Joy Amongst the Pines

Beneath tall pines where the sunlight streams,
Creatures giggle in their sunny dreams.
Breezes laugh as they dance and twirl,
Tickling leaves in a playful whirl.

A woodpecker taps in rhythmic cheer,
Echoing fun for all who hear.
Squirrels chatter in a fast-paced race,
Each one smiles, joy on its face.

The resin drips in a shining glow,
While nature's antics continue to flow.
Amidst the evergreens, leaps abound,
A joyous symphony, a splendid sound.

Mirthful Moments in Nature's Hold

In the heart of green where laughter sings,
Tiny feet scurry, oh what joy it brings!
A chipmunk teases a shy little mouse,
While hidden away, a smiling house.

With giggles carried by the wind's flight,
Wildflowers sway in sheer delight.
Fluffy clouds join in the fun parade,
Painting the sky as memories are made.

Beneath a sky so vast and bright,
Wonders blossom, a joyful sight.
In this playful realm, time stands still,
Mirth for the heart, a nature's thrill.

Connection Under the Treetops

In the shade where whispers meet,
Silly stories make us greet.
Beneath the branches, shadows play,
Friends in jest, we pass the day.

Tickles carried by the breeze,
Giggling like the buzzing bees.
Laughter floats like summer air,
Joyful hearts without a care.

Moments wrapped in light and grin,
Echoes where our fun begins.
Sunny smiles and carefree games,
In this space, we chase our flames.

Heartfelt Happy Moments

A sneaky squirrel steals a snack,
And giggles follow in its track.
Trees lean in, as if to hear,
The silly tales we've spun quite near.

Chasing shadows, we run free,
In our laughter, pure glee.
Beneath the sky, so vast and wide,
Our happiness, it just can't hide.

With every grin, the minutes fly,
Underneath that endless sky.
A canvas lit with joy and cheer,
In every moment, you are near.

Sunlit Shenanigans

When playful rays ignite our fun,
We dance around, every one.
Chasing laughs with light as guide,
In this game, we all abide.

Silly pranks and stories shared,
Each bright smile tells we cared.
In the warmth of golden beams,
We weave together all our dreams.

The world is bright, a magic show,
With every step, the joy will grow.
Sunlight paints our happy spree,
In this moment, we are free.

Laughter that Dances on the Wind

A zephyr whispers tales of joy,
Each chuckle rolls, a playful ploy.
Up in the branches, jesters hide,
With every rustle, fun is wide.

Windswept hair and vibrant cheers,
We share our hopes, we share our fears.
With every breeze, new jokes arise,
In laughter's echo, spirits rise.

Playful winds weave through the trees,
Frolicking while we bend our knees.
Together here, the world feels right,
As laughter dances, pure delight.

Whispers of Joy Beneath the Canopy

Tiny voices chatter and gleam,
As sunlight dances like a dream.
Silly shadows stretch and sway,
While giggles echo through the day.

Breezes tease with playful pranks,
Sprinkling cheer like happy yanks.
Laughter tickles every leaf,
Joyful moments, oh so brief.

Birds convene for a comedy show,
Chirping lines that steal the glow.
Around the trunks of emerald delight,
Smiles bloom like flowers, shining bright.

With every sway, a chuckle grows,
As nature's humor gently flows.
Underneath the grand embrace,
We find our refuge, our happy place.

Revelry in the Shade of Giants

Under wide branches, we find our cheer,
With every rustle, magic draws near.
The world spins in a whimsical dance,
Inviting us all to join in a prance.

Jokes told softly by the breeze,
Sweeping through the gently swaying leaves.
Echoes of laughter bounce so grand,
While sunlight draws patterns on the land.

Squirrels on branches, quite the jest,
Poking fun at their furry guests.
Ticklish whispers float in the air,
As smiles spread everywhere.

With every look to the towering trees,
The mood lifts high, hearts are at ease.
In the shade of giants, we find delight,
Bound together, everything feels right.

Giggling in the Embrace of Evergreen

Beneath the green where secrets spill,
We catch a thrill, we catch a chill.
The twinkling stars of evening light,
Curious creatures frolic and flight.

Wobbly branches sway with grace,
Tickling feet in this playful space.
The ground erupts with bursts of glee,
As laughter rings among the tree.

A gentle tug, a leaf takes flight,
Chasing giggles into the night.
Tiny critters join the fun,
In this paradise, joy's never done.

Nature's stage, we play our part,
Every moment, a work of art.
In the embrace of evergreen's sway,
We find our bliss, our bright array.

Chuckles Among the Branches

Branches arch like a joyful grin,
Where sparrows gossip, and fun begins.
With every rustle, mirth displayed,
A backyard party, a masquerade.

Mischievous bugs play peekaboo,
While sunlight hugs the morning dew.
Whispers trickle, soft and sweet,
As we share moments, our hearts repeat.

Under the boughs, we spin our tales,
Of daring adventures, and shimmering gales.
With laughter bouncing off every trunk,
In this vibrant haven, our spirits funk.

As shadows dance, so do we,
In the funhouse of the great old tree.
With chuckles stitched into the day,
We create memories that forever stay.

Glee Among the Tall Trunks

Beneath the towering trees, we play,
With shadows dancing, bright and gay.
Giggles mingle with chirps from the sky,
As squirrels chase each other, oh my!

The sun peeks through in a sneaky way,
Tickling our noses—what a cheeky play!
Branches sway to a whimsical tune,
While we spin around, like flowers in bloom.

A blanket spread, sandwiches delight,
We snack and chatter from morning to night.
Oh, how the clouds drift near and wide,
As we revel in joy, with a lighthearted glide.

In the embrace of nature's cheer,
Our laughter rings—so pure, so clear.
Each moment stolen in this sunny glade,
Eternal joy in the laughter we made.

Mirth in the Mossy Nook

Nestled in greens, we find our bliss,
Mossy patches beckon, we can't resist.
A toad hops by with a curious stare,
As we burst into giggles, unaware.

Jokes fly like kites in the warm, soft breeze,
Tickling our ribs, bringing us to our knees.
A ladybug lands, we name her Lou,
In this mossy nook, nothing feels new.

We race little ants in a silly old game,
Each tiny creature, we're all the same.
With a pop and a fizzle, our drinks overflow,
While we feign sorrow for such a fine show.

Time slips away like the breeze we chase,
In this nook of laughter, there's space to embrace.
Mirth fills the air, a soft, gentle hug,
Where joy sprouts anew, like a bright little bug.

Unwinding Happiness in the Shade

Under broad canopies, we stretch, we yawn,
Creating mischief from dusk till dawn.
The warmth of laughter hangs in the air,
With silly stories we're eager to share.

The leaves whisper secrets like old friends do,
As we plot and plan, something sparkly and new.
Our shadows tumble across the cool grass,
Each moment a treasure that we hope won't pass.

With a splash of water, and a giggly cheer,
We turn our ordinary days into cheer.
A gentle breeze carries our hearty song,
And the world feels perfect, where we all belong.

Laughter echoes beneath leafy gates,
In this hidden world, we celebrate fates.
With joy in our hearts and smiles alight,
We savor these moments, so pure and bright.

Radiant Moments in Rooted Realms

In a kingdom of trunks, where the sun does stream,
We weave our laughter into a dream.
A tumble, a trip, what a sight to behold,
As stories of folly bravely unfold.

The ground beneath us, a bouncy soft bed,
Like pillows of humor, where silliness spread.
We sketch funny faces on stumps that we find,
As nature chuckles, it surely is kind.

Chasing the clouds, we reach for the sky,
With each silly stance, we soar oh so high.
In this radiant realm, where happiness flows,
Every shared giggle like a flower that grows.

At dusk we gather, with stars shining bright,
Still spinning in laughter, a magical night.
In the roots of our joy, we find what is real,
In the moments together, our hearts learn to heal.

Frolics in the Forest

In a glen where shadows play,
Little critters bounce and sway.
Whispers hide behind the trees,
Tickles carried on the breeze.

Squirrels dance with acorn hats,
Rabbits jog with funny spats.
Breezy giggles fill the air,
Nature's pranksters everywhere.

Frogs wear crowns of dandelion,
Chasing flies, they leap in tryin'.
Rustling leaves hold secret jokes,
Mischief sparked by cheeky folks.

Underneath the leafy shade,
Joy erupts, no plans are made.
In this merry, leafy zone,
Laughter turns the woods to home.

Sunbeams and Smiles

Sunlight filters through the trees,
Casting sparkles with the breeze.
Flowers giggle at the sun,
Dancing petals, purest fun.

Bumblebees with tiny suits,
Buzzing songs in funny boots.
Each bright ray, a warm embrace,
Nature's joy, a laughing place.

Clouds drift by with silly faces,
Chasing time in playful races.
In this scene, where shadows beam,
Every moment feels like dream.

Glimmers catch the playful eye,
As butterflies flit and fly.
With every whim, the day's a prize,
In the light, the spirit lies.

Joyous Reverie Under Branches

Under branches, soft and wide,
Giggles echo, fears subside.
Children chase the fireflies' glow,
Moonlit paths where wild things flow.

Acorns tumble, games begun,
Underneath the laughing sun.
Pine cones roll, a playful race,
Joyful hearts in nature's space.

The wind whispers secrets sweet,
Tickling toes of tiny feet.
Jumps and shouts, a lively cheer,
Magic sprinkled everywhere.

Beneath the sky, so vast and blue,
Every moment feels brand new.
In these woods, we laugh and spring,
Joyous dreams are ours to bring.

Giggles Among the Pine Needles

Pine needles carpet the ground,
Where silly echoes can be found.
Bouncing laughter fills the air,
Nature's humor everywhere.

Twisting trees with knobby knees,
Whistle tunes that sway the leaves.
Tails of foxes brush the grass,
As playful shadows dance and pass.

Frolicking with wild delight,
Under stars that twinkle bright.
Raccoons wearing masks of fun,
Sneaky smiles in evening sun.

Joy spills forth from every nook,
Adventure waits in every book.
Among the pines, we find our glee,
In this realm, we're wild and free.

Revelry in the Rustling Boughs

In the shade where branches sway,
Squirrels dance and children play.
Tickling leaves with every breeze,
Joyful giggles float with ease.

A jester bird with feathered flair,
Perched above, a silly stare.
Chasing shadows, laughter sings,
Life is bright with silly things.

With acorns dropped like tiny bombs,
The ground shakes with playful qualms.
Nature's stage, a merry show,
Giggles burst, they ebb and flow.

In this realm of leafy cheer,
Every chuckle draws us near.
Follow trails of amber light,
Where joy reigns from morn till night.

Cheerful Glade

In a glade where sunbeams peek,
Bumbling bees begin to sneak.
Wobbling rabbits on the chase,
Silly antics, nature's grace.

A friendly breeze pulls leaves aside,
While butterflies take a wild ride.
Frolicking in the warming sun,
Moments shared, we laugh as one.

Under canopies of green delight,
We create our own soundtrack bright.
With every rustle, jokes align,
Creating laughter, pure and fine.

Sunset hues dance in our eyes,
As evening whispers soft goodbyes.
In every shadow, fun resides,
In this glade where joy abides.

Playful Shadows at Dusk

As daylight fades, the shadows play,
Stretching limbs, they dance away.
Whispers low, the night creeps in,
A playful spirit starts to spin.

Crickets chirp a lively tune,
Beneath the watch of glowing moon.
Here, we drag our doubts aside,
And ride the waves of joy and pride.

Frogs join in with leaps so grand,
While fireflies twinkle, hand in hand.
Echoes of laughter fill the air,
A giddy spirit, bright and rare.

In shadows long, the fun sets free,
Embracing all that's meant to be.
With every twinkle, we find cheer,
Reveling in what feels so dear.

Serenity and Splendor

Beneath the boughs where laughter swells,
A tapestry of joy compels.
With whispers soft and chuckles bright,
We gather 'neath the fading light.

Nature's joke in rustling leaves,
A gentle tickle that relieves.
Each rustle calls, a sweet surprise,
With every blink, a brand new guise.

Through dappled shades, our spirits soar,
Playful moments ask for more.
The heart's delight, a shining gem,
In harmony, we rise and stem.

And as the twilight steals the day,
In light's embrace, we choose to stay.
Serenity in joyful flight,
Where every giggle feels just right.

Cherished Times Under the Naturale

In the shade of leafy eyes,
We toss our cares to the skies.
With each giggle, the branches sway,
Nature's laughter leads the way.

Bouncing bugs jump to the beat,
Tickling toes and dancing feet.
Gather here, both near and far,
We carry joy like a bright star.

Hidden paths and secret nooks,
Filled with stories in worn books.
Whispers of fun come alive,
Each memory helps us thrive.

As shadows play on the ground,
In every chuckle, love is found.
Time stands still within this space,
In nature's arms, we find our place.

Echoes of Delight Amidst the Moss

Mossy cushions cradle our feet,
With joy that feels so sweet.
A frog jumps by with a mighty 'plop,'
Our laughter makes the still air stop.

Squirrels prance with a cheeky grin,
While we share tales of where we've been.
Every chuckle, a melody,
Nature sings in harmony.

Under the canopy, we find our cheer,
With every joke, we draw all near.
Breezy whispers may tease the trees,
But our happiness flows like the breeze.

As twilight wraps its arms around,
Each giggle leaves a magic sound.
In this lush world, joy surely thrives,
Memories here will come alive.

Serenity Wrapped in Green

In emerald folds, we drift and dream,
Together we form a playful team.
Beneath the boughs, we dare to play,
A symphony of laughter leads the way.

With crickets serenading the night,
Our hearts are light, our spirits bright.
A friendly breeze begins to tease,
Spreading mirth among the leaves.

We wander paths adorned with cheer,
Every tree holds a story dear.
The whispers of the rustling ferns,
Echo back what our heart yearns.

So let's embrace this vibrant scene,
And weave our tales in shades of green.
In every smile, the world feels free,
Nature's embrace is where we'll be.

Happy Trails in the Timber

Along the trail where laughter plays,
Every moment, a bright array.
The trees sway gently, tapping toes,
In this forest where friendship grows.

Each step we take, the world feels new,
Every turn brings a view or two.
With nature's brush, we sketch our fun,
Dancing shadows, the day's not done.

Frolicking through the sunlit haze,
We share our joys in silly ways.
A dance-off with the woodland crew,
Who knew trees could entertain too?

As dusk drapes its fabric around,
Our laughter echoes, a warming sound.
In this timber where spirits rise,
We find delight in the wild's guise.

Harmony of Laughter in the Grove

In the shade where shadows play,
Squirrels dance in bright array,
Chirping birds break into song,
Nature hums, it won't be long.

Tickled leaves with gentle breeze,
Fluffy clouds like butter cheese,
A merry chase on soft, green ground,
Joyous echoes all around.

A mischievous breeze, a fluttering hat,
The bounding pup, imagine that!
Giggling friends with sun-kissed cheeks,
Collecting tales that laughter speaks.

As the sun sets, rosy hues,
In the grove, we'll share our views,
With every chuckle, bonds will glow,
In the harmony, our spirits flow.

Fun Times in the Sun-dappled Haven

Beneath the branches, playtime thrives,
Bouncing balls and swinging lives,
A picnic spread with treats galore,
We munch and tell tales, wanting more.

A playful breeze with mischief weaves,
Tugging at hats and leaf-worn sleeves,
Sticky fingers on sweet delight,
Giggling til we bid goodnight.

Scavenger hunts, our laughter grows,
Hiding treasures where no one knows,
A tumble here, a splash there too,
In this haven, skies are blue.

When the stars peek through the leaves,
We gather close and share our dreams,
With silly jokes and laughter clear,
In our haven, all is cheer.

Whispers of Woodland Joy

In the woods where giggles bloom,
Whispers chase away the gloom,
Frolicking fairies, tiny and spry,
Fluttering wings as they zoom by.

With acorns scattered, games begin,
Rolling laughter, cheeky grins,
Wildflowers sway, nodding in agreement,
In this space, time feels like a treat.

A rustling sound, a playful cat,
Trying to catch a bouncing hat,
Silly stories shared with glee,
Everyone's heart is light and free.

At dusk, the fireflies dance around,
Painting joy upon the ground,
With each glimmer, we unite,
In woodland whispers, pure delight.

Mirth Beneath the Canopy

Underneath the leafy veil,
Laughter drifts, a gentle sail,
A gathering of friends, bright and bold,
Sharing secrets yet untold.

A raccoon peaks with curious eyes,
While butterflies perform their flies,
Tickling feet on soft mossy trails,
Life unfolds with amusing tales.

Chasing shadows, spinning round,
With every tumble, joy is found,
Even the trees seem to grin,
As we play on without chagrin.

The sun dips low, the sky a flame,
Yet in this moment, none are the same,
With laughter echoing, spirits soar,
Beneath the canopy, we want more.

Chortles in the Shade

Beneath the branches, shadows play,
Frolicsome whispers of the day.
A squirrel drops acorns with a thud,
And giggles burst with every thud.

Breezes tease the tree's old curls,
Tickling flowers, making them twirl.
A rabbit hops, a funny sight,
Dancing in the soft twilight.

Friends gather round, with joy they share,
Stories that spiral through the air.
With every chuckle, spirits grow,
In this sweet haven, laughter flows.

As twilight falls and stars appear,
The joy remains, it's crystal clear.
Under the boughs, where hearts unite,
Chortles linger throughout the night.

Glee Among the Tall Trees

Up in the branches, chipmunks race,
With tiny feet, they find their place.
A crow caws jokes, the punchline's loud,
And every twig holds back a crowd.

Sunlight dapples on the ground,
While froggy hops make a funny sound.
A bee wears glasses, looking quite smart,
Buzzing around, a quirky part.

Picnic spreads, with laughter laid,
Sandwiches piled, all home-crafted.
With every bite and silly cheer,
Glee erupts, loud and clear.

As shadows stretch, the fun won't cease,
In this grove, there's pure release.
The laughter lingers, and so it stays,
Among the tall trees, in playful ways.

Harmony of Hearts in the Grove

In the grove where the laughter sings,
Dancing daisies wear shiny rings.
The butterfly flutters, a silly old thing,
As chubby toads pretend to swing.

Beneath the boughs, an echo sounds,
That wraps around like playful hounds.
A kitten sneezes and tumbles down,
Creating chuckles all around.

Friends sway together, hand in hand,
With every joke, they make a stand.
The sunlight flickers, a winking star,
While mischief races, no one stays far.

As daylight fades, their giggles grow,
A harmony only they could know.
Hearts entwined, with joyful throes,
In this sweet grove, their spirit glows.

Echoes of Laughter Through Leaves

In the clearing, sounds of cheer,
Branches sway, and all draw near.
A monkey drops his fruity stash,
And with a wink, he makes a splash.

The breeze carries whispers, so sweet,
Tickling cheeks and dancing feet.
A dog chases shadows with a bark,
In this lively realm where laughter sparks.

Friends share stories, whimsy unfolds,
With playful tricks, mischief bold.
Every twinkle in the trees,
Echoes laughter, a gentle breeze.

As stars appear, the giggles rise,
With glimmering moons and starry skies.
Echoes of joy will surely remain,
Amidst the trees, where fun's unchained.

Jovial Spirits in Nature's Arms

In the woods where giggles flow,
The trees sway with a gentle show.
Squirrels dance on branches high,
While breezes hum a merry sigh.

Underneath the shade of green,
Frolics and pranks burst on the scene.
A chorus of laughter fills the air,
With whispers of joy everywhere.

Dandelions wave, their heads so bright,
As shadows play, oh what a sight!
With mischief lurking in every nook,
All nature's misfits share a laugh book.

Daisies chuckle in colorful troops,
Amidst the winks of woodland loops.
Every rustle brings a new delight,
In this realm where spirits ignite.

Merriment in the Timberlands

A woodpecker drums a funny beat,
While rabbits hop on tiny feet.
The pinecones giggle as they drop,
In this playful, leafy backdrop.

Sunbeams twirl in a playful dance,
Inviting whispers, a cheerful chance.
Amidst the trunks, friendships bloom,
In nature's laughter, there's always room.

Chipmunks play tag in wild arrays,
With silly stunts that brighten the days.
Leaves rustle, sharing secret jokes,
Amongst the giggling, teasing folks.

A squirrel's tail twitches with delight,
As shadows stretch in fading light.
In this timberland where joy's awoken,
The spirit of fun remains unspoken.

Delight in the Dappled Shade

Whispers weave through branches tall,
As sunlight giggles in a gentle sprawl.
The bumblebees buzz in jolly swirls,
While nature spins and twirls with pearls.

A hedgehog's snicker, a fox's grin,
Among the ferns, where joys begin.
Each curving path leads to shared glee,
With echoes of laughter sung by the trees.

Bright mushrooms peek from leafy beds,
As woodland secrets dance in threads.
In this mosaic of playful hues,
Every moment gives rise to muse.

Morning dew glistens like a jest,
In the dappled shade, we find our quest.
With chuckles and tales that never fade,
In this canvas of kinship, laughter's made.

Jests Beneath the Green Canopy

Beneath the leaves, the tricksters play,
In a world where worries melt away.
Giggling critters share their plights,
Under the canopy of blushing lights.

An acorn tries to roll up high,
But tumbles down with a cheerful sigh.
Nearby, the frogs croak silly tunes,
As sunshine splits the afternoon.

With every rustle, the fun persists,
Nature's blend of secret twists.
In this grove where joy is rife,
Friendships flourish, bringing life.

A kerfuffle starts, a lively chase,
With sprightly steps in a joyous race.
Every moment bursts with glee,
In the haven where hearts dance free.

Unfurling Joy Among the Greenery

Beneath the branches, whispers play,
Nature's jesters bring bright day.
A squirrel dances, quite absurd,
As birdies chirp, a lively herd.

With every rustle, laughter grows,
A ticklish breeze, as joy bestows.
The flowers sway in silly glee,
Their petals twirl, wild and free.

Around the roots, mischief thrives,
In this green realm, humor thrives.
Each shadow casts a playful glance,
Inviting all to join the dance.

So gather here, your cares away,
In nature's arms, let spirits sway.
A tapestry of smiles will weave,
In this bright haven, tricks perceive.

Spirit of Frolic in Nature's Nest

In the boughs where joy does scheme,
The sunlight spills, a golden beam.
A cheeky rabbit hops with flair,
Tickling fawns with gentle air.

The leaves above are giggling bright,
As shadows dance, a silly sight.
Mushrooms laugh in polka dots,
While critters wear their funniest spots.

Ripe strawberries blush in delight,
As bees buzz past, a comic flight.
Each step reveals a new surprise,
As nature winks with vibrant eyes.

So come and play where wonders grow,
In this nest, let humor flow.
From dusk till dawn, let laughter reign,
A spirit bright, with no disdain.

Play and Ponder in the Pines

In the pines, where shadows tease,
Laughter echoes on the breeze.
A fox in socks spins 'round and round,
While giggling birds hop on the ground.

The clouds above play a game of chase,
As sunbeams tickle every face.
A woodpecker taps a silly tune,
With every beat, the flowers swoon.

Rolling hills invite a race,
As children tumble in a happy space.
The playful brook joins the fun,
Splashing logs in the warming sun.

Moments here are light and free,
Filled with joy, rich as can be.
So linger long, let spirits soar,
In this pine haven, forevermore.

Gentle Giggles Among the Flora

Among the blooms, a riddle stirs,
Where daisies play with flitting furs.
A butterfly poses with a grin,
As ants parade, a conga line begins.

The gentle breeze whispers a jest,
As blossoms sway, they're at their best.
A sleepy caterpillar grumbles loud,
While bees debate, an amusing crowd.

The grass holds secrets of silly cheer,
As frogs croak tales for all to hear.
The sunlight dapples, a playful dance,
Inviting all to take a chance.

So sit awhile, let laughter bloom,
In every corner, banish gloom.
With every petal, joy expands,
In this sweet refuge where fun commands.

Rapture in the Ripples of Green

Beneath the trees, a dance begins,
Where shadows play and giggles spin.
The grass tickles toes in the gentle breeze,
As whispers swirl with teasing ease.

A squirrel leaps with a cheeky flair,
While robins chirp their tunes to share.
Laughter rings through the vibrant scene,
In a world so bright, so fresh, so green.

With each turn, a surprise appears,
Rolling down hills, there's nothing to fear.
Nature lifts spirits, ignites the soul,
In the jests of today, we find our role.

Through rapturous moments, joy is sown,
In a tapestry where mirth is grown.
We skip and hop, with heartbeats keen,
In this paradise, forever serene.

Sweet Singsong Under the Arching Boughs

In the shade where fun takes flight,
With tunes that twirl in morning light.
A rabbit hops, all fluff and yelp,
Chasing shadows with a playful help.

Under branches, whispers soar,
As Nature giggles, we want more.
Each melody, a giggle shared,
Under the boughs, where hearts are bared.

The brook babbles with clever ease,
Telling tales of the dancing leaves.
Awash in rapture, we twirl and spin,
In this symphony, we all join in.

Around each turn, a jest unfolds,
In pathways paved with soft, bright golds.
We wear our laughter like a gown,
In the sweetest singsong, we won't drown.

Nature's Jests in the Glade

In a glade where shadows tease,
A fox lays low, a trickster's ease.
Every rustle hides a grin,
As antics burst, we're pulled right in.

The sun peeks through with a cheeky gaze,
While flowers sway in a joyful haze.
Each fluttering wing tells a sly delight,
From dawn until the end of night.

A dance of leaves in the gentle air,
Teasing secrets they love to share.
A world alive with wit and charm,
Wraps us close, safe from harm.

Every step reveals a fun-filled jest,
In nature's realm, we are the guests.
With every laugh, our troubles fade,
In this joyful place, we're unafraid.

Gathered Gleeful Souls Amongst the Trees

Amid the woods, the laughter flows,
With every step, a joy that grows.
Chasing shadows and flickering sights,
In the dance of days and the cool, soft nights.

A gathering of souls, hearts leap high,
With whispers that flutter, a joyous sigh.
We weave through the trunks, spirits unchained,
In this miracle where we're unrestrained.

With every giggle, the branches sway,
As friendship blossoms in wild display.
We celebrate all that makes us bright,
Underneath the canopy, in shared delight.

So here we stand, happy and free,
In this realm where we long to be.
Each moment cherished, life like a breeze,
Gathered, we dance, surrounded by trees.

Harmonious Echoes in the Forest

Beneath the boughs where shadows play,
The squirrels dance in bright display.
With nutty jokes that crack the air,
Their chittering laughter everywhere.

A fox in boots, so sly and spry,
Tells tales of mischief, oh my my!
The birds join in with songs so sweet,
While petals fall with rhythmic beat.

A deer prances with a soft glance,
Mistaking a twig for pants to prance.
The laughter swells, a gentle tide,
While trees lean in to share their pride.

In this grove, joy comes alive,
With playful hearts, creatures thrive.
A merry band in nature's den,
Where giggles echo now and then.

Watercolors of Wit in the Woods

Dappled light on grassy sheets,
Where every corner hides new treats.
A bear in shades, with style untold,
Shares puns like honey, sweet and bold.

The rabbits hop in vibrant hues,
Swapping stories, old and new.
With splashes of mirth across the scene,
Each chuckle brightens, sharp and keen.

A hedgehog sports a tiny hat,
A sight that makes you giggle flat.
With quills of joy, he sets the pace,
In nature's gallery, a smiling face.

As clouds drift by and shadows shift,
Their playful antics are a gift.
In this forest, joy is spun,
With every joke, the day is won.

Soothing Rhythms of Joy

In the glen where laughter flows,
The breeze carries the jest that glows.
With whispers soft among the leaves,
A chorus bright that never grieves.

The chipmunks chat with tiny glee,
Sharing secrets, wild and free.
The chorus of frogs joins in the fun,
Their ribbits dance beneath the sun.

A dance of shadows, light and grace,
As chuckles weave through nature's lace.
Where mischief blooms in every nook,
And life unfolds a joyful book.

A giggling brook adds to the cheer,
Its bubbling voice, for all to hear.
In this realm where spirits play,
The rhythms hold the world at bay.

A Festival of Feathers and Fun

High above on branches thick,
Parrots gossip, oh so quick.
In plumage bright, they steal the show,
With puns and jests that swiftly flow.

Fluffy owls, wise yet spry,
With owl-credible jokes, oh my!
They hoot with glee in twilight's light,
Turning the dusk into delight.

A peacock struts, all tails ablaze,
With every step, the forest sways.
As friends from nests join in the throng,
A playful vibe where we belong.

The festival swells, a vibrant sight,
With feathers floating in the night.
In this party, hearts unite,
Dancing till dawn, what pure delight!

www.ingramcontent.com/pod-product-compliance
Lightning Source LLC
Chambersburg PA
CBHW051643160426
43209CB00004B/767